Richard Rogers
Inside Out

Richard Rogers
Inside Out

Royal
Academy
of Arts

First published on the occasion of the exhibition 'Richard Rogers RA: Inside Out'

Royal Academy of Arts, London
18 July–13 October 2013

The Royal Academy of Arts is grateful to Her Majesty's Government for agreeing to indemnify this exhibition under the National Heritage Act 1980, and to Resource, The Council for Museums, Archives and Libraries, for its help in arranging the indemnity.

Exhibition curators
Jeremy Melvin
Sarah Gaventa

Exhibition organisation
Nicole Ruegsegger

Photographic and copyright co-ordination
Christos Ioannidis

Publication
Royal Academy Publications:
Beatrice Gullström
Alison Hissey
Elizabeth Horne
Carola Krueger
Peter Sawbridge
Nick Tite

Project editors:
Tom Neville, Vicky Wilson

Design:
Esterson Associates

Colour origination:
Zanardi

Printed in Italy by Zanardi

British Library Cataloguing-in-Publication Data
A catalogue record for this book is available from the British Library.

ISBN 978-1-907533-61-7 (standard edition)
ISBN 978-1-907533-76-1 (limited edition)

Distributed outside the United States and Canada by Thames & Hudson Ltd, London

Distributed in the United States and Canada by Harry N. Abrams, Inc., New York

Acknowledgements
The publishers of this book would like to express their gratitude to the following individuals for their invaluable assistance:

Ricky Burdett
Michael Craig-Martin
Robert Fiehn
Sarah Gaventa
Jennifer Goldsmith
Michael Heseltine
Vicki MacGregor
Jeremy Melvin
Jo Murtagh
Camilla Nicholls
Nicolai Ouroussoff
Anne Power
Richard Rogers

Front cover:
Richard Rogers RA, portrait by Andrew Zuckerman

Back cover: Piano + Rogers, Centre Pompidou, Paris, 1971–77, detail of services and structure on the building's east face

Page 2: Richard Rogers Partnership, Lloyd's of London, 1978–86, view down into The Room

Contents

President's Foreword

Opposite: Richard Rogers Partnership, 'Design for Manufacture', concept sketch. A radical attempt to design factory-produced, energy-efficient housing as a response to a government-backed competition

Overleaf: Richard Rogers Partnership, Oxley Woods, 2007, the first of the 'Design for Manufacture' competition winners to be built

Architects have played an important part in the Royal Academy ever since it was founded. 'Richard Rogers RA: Inside Out', marking his eightieth birthday and half a century in practice, helps to explain why architecture is an integral part of an academy of arts, and how it adds a dimension to painting, sculpture and print-making.

Both book and exhibition convey the range of Rogers's creative activity, from politics and sociology to the aesthetic concerns he shares with contemporary artists (he lives among paintings by Philip Guston, Cy Twombly, Andy Warhol and many others). Architects inevitably come into contact with politics: Rogers has probably taken this further than any other, as a social campaigner and active member of the House of Lords, but most importantly in how his designs give aesthetic expression to his social and political beliefs. Architecture makes human activity an integral part of aesthetic experience, but in Rogers's hands art and everyday life constantly interweave, challenging and redefining each other.

This is apparent throughout the exhibition, but the pre-fabricated house which will be erected in the Burlington House courtyard in early August will make this explicit. It is an example of a system called 'Design for Manufacture', the latest of Rogers's attempts to provide high-quality housing for a low cost.

A member of the Royal Academy since 1978, Rogers's own life combines the social, political and cultural. This makes him a very suitable subject for our first architectural exhibition in Burlington Gardens, and our first large-scale exploration of the work of a living architect since 1998. In the years since, we have developed a vibrant Architecture Programme of lectures, discussions and small exhibitions, helping to fulfil our goal to be a place where the arts are debated and made as well as displayed. We hope this exhibition will set a pattern for the future.

We are very grateful to Richard and Ruthie Rogers, and to his colleagues at Rogers Stirk Harbour + Partners, as well as to our sponsors, Ferrovial Agroman, Heathrow and Laing O'Rourke, for their help in mounting the exhibition.

Christopher Le Brun PRA, President, Royal Academy of Arts

Introduction
Jeremy Melvin

Saved in the Rogers Stirk Harbour + Partners' archive is a sequence of diagrams that explains the concept for the National Assembly for Wales in Cardiff. The first shows water and sky with an implied line for land – the site's three elemental conditions; the second depicts how the land is adapted into a floor of rising horizontal levels with a roof above; the final one demonstrates how roof and sky, and land and floor, can be brought into taut and charged relationships with each other to create a series of routes, views and spaces. The concept becomes, in a phrase Richard Rogers first used in describing the aims of the Centre Pompidou in Paris but which forms a constant thread throughout his work, 'a place for all people'.

This simple drawing contains some of the most important aspects of Richard Rogers's thinking. It is, typically, a collaborative exercise, since it was almost certainly drawn by Ivan Harbour, the partner who led the project and was responsible for absorbing and developing the ideas and influences around it and turning them into a building. The drawing also shows how nature is present but adapted to human need, as daylight and fresh air flow through the structure. People are able to meet each other in various formal and informal settings, and as some of those people may be mandated with political responsibility, the building sets the stage for encounters between ordinary people and power.

Rogers's architecture is far too complex to convey through a single diagram. It incorporates a vast array of influences drawn from across the spectrum of culture and politics as well as from the extensive networks and collaborations which have informed and delivered his work throughout his professional life. Just as the National Assembly for Wales drawing only scratches the surface of Rogers's thought, it also hints at a much larger collegial process by which ideas are developed into buildings.

Explaining how this creative process works is the aim of the exhibition 'Richard Rogers RA: Inside Out'. It starts by introducing visitors to Rogers's way of thinking, his ethos. It moves on to unravel a series of themes that run through many of his projects, old and new, large and small. It concludes with a section on 'the power of the city', a phrase that conveys the importance of urban life and culture within his work. For Rogers, power is about enfranchising the collective rather than a concentration in the hands of an elite.

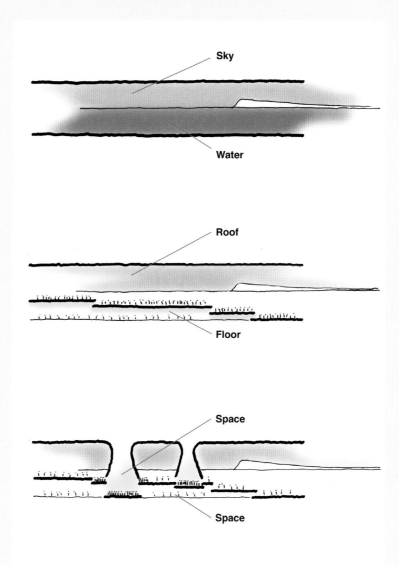

Richard Rogers
Partnership, National
Assembly for Wales,
Cardiff, 1988–2005,
concept diagrams

Pages 14–15:
Richard Rogers
Partnership, National
Assembly for Wales,
entrance. Public spaces
are raised above the
bay on a plinth that
rises from the waterside,
allowing daylight
to penetrate the
administrative spaces,
which are sheltered
under a lightweight,
undulating roof

Architecture inevitably combines ethics and aesthetics. Rogers has embraced the challenge of that combination and explored how its two components drive each other forward. He chose architecture as a profession partly because it offered opportunities to address social concerns. He frequently reminds his colleagues, clients and audiences that 'architecture is a social and political art.' He believes the social and political cannot exist in isolation from one another, which in turn underpins his conviction that art in general and architecture in particular have an obligation to be of their time, to use contemporary imagery, methods and technology.

To develop and deliver these ideas Rogers has had to push the conventional boundaries of architectural practice. Architecture has always been collaborative – Stonehenge and the great Gothic cathedrals, for instance, are hardly products of single individuals – but Rogers's belief in a collaborative approach is profound. While his dyslexia and reticence about drawing may have given some impetus to viewing a collegial approach as desirable, there is an overarching belief that interesting and exciting work results from the interaction of ideas from all quarters. Strategies familiar in contemporary art but less so in architecture, such as chance and indeterminacy, also became hallmarks of his practices' creative process.

The potential power derived from collaboration also underlies Rogers's commitment to urbanism. Cities originated, he points out, in the need for co-operation, and demonstrated that a co-operating community was much more than the sum of its individuals. Technology, from simple hand tools to the most sophisticated computers, is similarly valuable because it extends a single person's capabilities beyond his or her immediate limitations. Humanism and technology are, for Rogers, closely related.

At the start of the 1980s his practice developed a unique constitution that enshrines ideas about community, teamwork, equity, collaboration and social responsibility. Comments from his notebook at the time set out the goals: 'common ownership' and 'transfer of ownership by way of self-denying ideas', 'prosperity = teamwork = not security for the chosen few or dictatorial powers', 'bosses and staff division questioned'. This page concludes, 'wealth like power corrupts and provokes greed + envy – no real

Richard Rogers with 'London as it could be' at the 'Foster Rogers Stirling' exhibition, Royal Academy of Arts, London, 1986

community can be formed.' Underlying the constitution are two of Rogers's fundamental beliefs: the need for community and the pernicious effect of greed. The constitution establishes a means of decision-making and of providing intellectual and organisational leadership without stifling initiative or tying it to undue financial reward, or 'security for the chosen few'.

Rogers's notebooks reveal his desire to practise architecture in a way that is ethical and humane. The constitution codifies that ethical humanism; it prohibits, for example, work associated with war or processes which cause excessive environmental pollution. Its writing also marked a point when the practice became more stable, allowing Rogers to initiate a series of significant and influential projects that focused on the relationship between politics, architecture and the city. One of the first was 'London as it could be', shown at the Royal Academy of Arts in 1986; the Walter Neurath Memorial Lecture, 'Architecture: A Modern View', followed in 1990; *A New London: Two Views*, co-authored with Labour MP Mark Fisher, came out in time for the 1992 General Election; and Rogers gave the Reith Lectures in 1995, which were published as *Cities for a Small Planet*. The Neurath lecture was an elegant and erudite exposition of architectural aesthetics as a product of ethical thought and the harnessing of modern technology for human benefit; *A New London* made the link between politics and urbanism explicit; the Reith Lectures analysed and explained Rogers's thinking about cities in general, showing how well-designed and well-governed cities, using appropriate technology, could provide environmentally sustainable living conditions as well as offering a frame for contemporary lifestyles.

Simultaneously Rogers became the first chair of the Architecture Foundation and took a leading role in developing the series of great public debates it organised in the spring and summer of 1996, the same year that he gained a formal political role as a member of the House of Lords. His work chairing the Urban Task Force started the following year and received cross-party support on the delivery of its reports. This personal programme of campaigning and socially responsible activity continues with, most recently, a resounding House of Lords speech, political lobbying and press articles on the need for proper planning controls to protect both the UK's green belt and one of

Filippo Brunelleschi's
dome for Florence
Cathedral, 1436

Rogers's abiding passions – the compact, sustainable city.

Rogers considers the work his team delivered through the Urban Task Force to be among his most significant achievements. The initiative brought together a range of people who were concerned with the physical environment – from academics, planners and politicians to developers and architects – and its 106 recommendations covered a wide spectrum of urban, economic and social conditions. It resulted in a rise from 50% to 80% of development taking place on redundant industrial – brownfield – land and an increase of average density by 30%. As Rogers points out, after a century of being shunned as a place to live for those who have choice, the city once more became attractive.

Family and environment are two influences Rogers cites above all others. He was born in Florence in 1933 and his early years were spent in a flat with a spectacular view of Filippo Brunelleschi's cathedral dome, an unquestioned masterpiece of the Renaissance, and a fine collection of the latest Modernist furniture. These pieces were a gift from his father's cousin, Ernesto Rogers, who was just beginning to make a name for himself as a Modernist architect and who would become an important figure in post-war Italian cultural life. While it would be simplistic to trace characteristics in Richard Rogers's own architecture from these formative influences, he was at least aware of the possibilities inherent in the juxtapositions of people, ideas, cultures and the artefacts that represent them.

His parents moved in 1939 from the warmth and affluence of Italy to an economically and spatially constrained life in London as it was preparing for war. Rogers describes his early impression of England in one word: 'hell'.

If the move to England relegated the rich cultural openness of Italy to a series of memories, it drew out another fundamental aspect of Rogers's ethos: fairness. His experiences of arbitrary discipline and unimaginative teaching as a boarder at an English prep school awakened a sense of fair play and rebellion at injustice. His Italian roots quickly labelled him as an 'enemy' and his status as an outsider was reinforced by his struggle with literacy. It was only in the 1970s, when his sons faced similar difficulties, that the condition of dyslexia was diagnosed.

However unpleasant Rogers found school, it brought out some of his strengths and helped to focus his interests. First, as he

Top: Ernesto Rogers, Sanatorium, Legnano, Italy, 1938

Bottom: BBPR (Ernesto Rogers and Enrico Peressutti), Torre Velasca, Milan, 1956–57

remembers it, he was large and so could defend himself. Second, it became apparent that he was 'a natural gang leader' and 'a very good boy scout, my first success!' Third, especially as the 1945 General Election brought the Labour Party to power at the end of the war and 'everybody at that time had socialist ideals, even the Conservatives', the possibility of a new society opened before him. As a doctor, his father was working in the nascent National Health Service and they discussed its ideals together.

Once it became possible to travel to Italy again after 1945, and as Rogers was growing into an adult, his unusual breadth of experience expanded into a far wider perceptual range than that of most of his peers. He *knew* life could be better than it was in post-war Britain, which meant that the Labour government's goal of a Welfare State was worth pursuing. In Italy, aesthetic and social experience could merge in the public realm. In Britain, if such a combination were possible, it was likely to be behind the iron railings of London's more exclusive squares or within the even more private realm of Oxford and Cambridge quadrangles. Rogers's concepts of fairness, openness to new ideas, and public space began to form and intertwine.

Spending time in Ernesto Rogers's young and cosmopolitan studio encouraged a feel for architecture, and Richard won a place at the Architectural Association, the only unashamedly Modernist school of architecture in Britain in the early 1950s. He remembers that his first essay divided his tutors – as well as marking his interest in cities. For his final design project he chose a school for difficult children, thoroughly researching how children's homes worked and perhaps more importantly throwing himself into an activity that really could make a difference to society and serve people who, like himself, did not fit easily into the system. His experience turned him away from a coercive or deterministic architecture to one where individuals can select their own level of engagement. Flexible and indeterminate space became an important interest and tutors such as Alan Colquhoun, John Killick and Peter Smithson helped Rogers to formulate a conception of architecture around his own thoughts and ambitions.

Moving temporarily to the US as a Fulbright Scholar at Yale provided new aesthetic experiences to add to his emerging appreciation of how architecture could serve society. The architectural historian Vincent Scully fired an enthusiasm for

Team 4 with Tony Hunt, engineer of many of their projects. Left to right: (back) Tony Hunt, Frank Peacock; (front) Aline Storry, Wendy Foster, Richard Rogers, Su Rogers, Norman Foster, Maurice Philips

Frank Lloyd Wright, which led Richard, his wife Su Rogers, who was studying city planning, and his classmate Norman Foster to travel around the US to visit Wright's buildings. With its four corner towers containing services for a 'non-specific' space in the centre, the Larkin Building in Buffalo seemed to predate by 50 years their ideas for served and servant spaces, as well as Rogers's own emerging interest in heavily serviced but ultimately flexible space. Other important influences from this time which remain with him are Russian Constructivism – he and Su lived with Naum Gabo, a friend of her parents – and the visionary technologist Buckminster Fuller.

They also discovered impressive industrial plants. In Britain an aesthetic derived from industrial construction seemed stuck in the nineteenth century, with railway sheds and the Crystal Palace. What they found in America was 'more immediate, being built at that time'. In Raphael Soriano, designer of one of the legendary California Case Study houses, Rogers discovered an architect who could use standard industrial products like I-beams as-found, rather than turning them into a new Doric order as Mies van der Rohe was doing. If the goal was to create architecture to serve a new society, then industry, industrial products and aesthetic strategies for using them might help to express that goal.

Many of the constituents of Rogers's ethos were taking shape. His family, of course, had always been there but he was developing an appreciation of the support he could give to and receive from a wider network of friends, colleagues and collaborators. His ideas of injustice and fairness had also taken root early, but the prevalence of socialist thought and action in the post-war period lent them sophistication while the Architectural Association helped to focus them into architectural thinking. And if the presence of Modernist furniture and view of Brunelleschi's dome had introduced him to the juxtaposition of modern and historic artefacts, his experience in the US, then both optimistic and unquestionably the most modern place in the world, had opened new aesthetic horizons. The next challenge was to forge all this into a way of practising architecture.

The opportunity arose when Su Rogers's parents asked the young couple to design a house. Team 4 was formed with Norman Foster and two of Rogers's close friends, Wendy Cheesman and her older sister Georgie Wolton, the only fully qualified

Team 4, Creek Vean,
Fiock, Cornwall,
1961–66, sketch

Creek Vean. Designed
for Su Rogers's parents,
the house has two wings
divided by a cascading
external stair leading
down to the boathouse
and creek

Creek Vean. The combined
kitchen/dining room, top,
is the heart of the house.
The bedrooms and office
in the northern wing are
connected by a top-lit
gallery, bottom

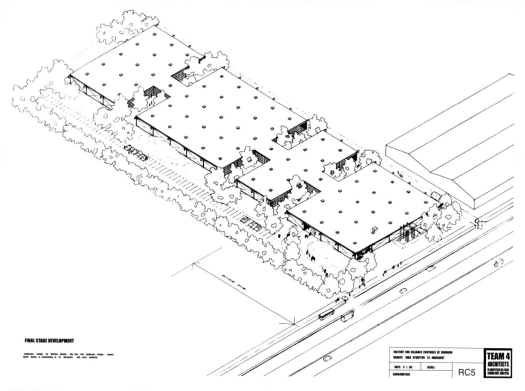

Team 4, Reliance Controls
factory, Swindon, 1967,
axonometic and external
detail. The building
used a simple but
elegant structural system
that allowed for future
expansion

Richard Rogers and Renzo Piano on the escalators at the Centre Pompidou

architect among them. She soon withdrew and Su Rogers took her place. The house, Creek Vean, is a masterpiece of sophisticated domestic design, conjuring a series of internal and external spaces to accommodate the clients' significant collection of modern art – they sold a Mondrian to pay for the building – as well as everyday living. But it also took five architects five years to build and its cost exceeded the Mondrian sale price, leading them to conclude that it was hardly a model for meeting the country's housing needs.

Their next significant project, a low-cost factory for Reliance Controls in Swindon completed in 1967, used steel posts, beams, profiled cladding and tight cross-bracing. They received the commission on the recommendation of James Stirling. Equally successful aesthetically, it was far more so in social and economic terms because it met the low budget, provided for change and expansion, and introduced the then revolutionary idea of workers and managers using the same entrance. But just as aesthetic and social programmes began to align, Norman and Wendy Foster, as she became after they married, left to found Foster Associates. Although some very talented architects worked for Team 4, including Rogers's long-term colleagues John Young, Laurie Abbott and Marco Goldschmied, there was barely enough work to hold the practice together. Even the arrival of Renzo Piano did not immediately lift their prospects, though winning the Centre Pompidou competition a year later certainly did. But it also posed a series of challenges to Rogers's attempt to practise as an ethical humanist architect.

Initially repulsed by the idea of a centralised cultural centre that would become a monument to a president, Rogers had opposed entering the competition. But gradually the task began to seem worthwhile. It provided an extraordinarily high-profile opportunity to demonstrate ideas about public space, indeterminacy, industrial production and an aesthetic derived from these changeable factors. The recent history of political protest in Paris in 1968 and its spread to other parts of the western world implied a reconfiguration of power, and, of particular interest to Rogers, questioned the role public space could play within this. The problem of conceiving a new cultural institution for an emerging spatial and social order was a worthy challenge.

The scale would demand teamwork and collaboration beyond anything Team 4 had envisaged. The practice expanded and took on talented designers such as Alan Stanton, who worked on Pompidou, and Jan Kaplicky, who worked on a series of other projects. It also began its ongoing collaboration with the engineers Arup Associates. Ted Happold in the initial stages, but in particular Peter Rice and Lennart Grut, made major contributions to the design. Rice was the engineer for many of Rogers's most significant projects until his tragically early death in 1992, while Grut became a director of Rogers's firm.

As the project unfolded it brought contact with people who understood the levers of political power, such as the client Robert Bordaz, a judge who had overseen the French withdrawal from Vietnam. Having credibility and the ear of the president helped to steer the radical and innovative scheme to fruition. There were also end-users of the calibre of the curator Pontus Hultén, who directed the museum of modern art which moved into the centre, and the composer Pierre Boulez, who was being lured back to France through the construction of the experimental centre for musical research, IRCAM, which formed part of the scheme. This pair of sophisticated cultural operators shared many of Rogers's aesthetic interests, including the relationship between contemporary art and technology, indeterminacy, and the recognition that everyday sights and sounds could be part of art.

The Centre Pompidou demonstrated the power of the architecture Rogers and his collaborators could produce. It showed how a strong concept – the idea of vast, column-free spaces stacked on top of each other and serviced to meet almost any purpose – could stay in focus, with contingent technical problems being solved around it. It was also a marker of Rogers's commitment to the prominence of public space. He refers to it as a place, not a building.

But it was not an automatic passport to more work, and even the core team began to fragment. Towards the end of 1977, however, a commission galvanised another phase of development: Lloyd's of London.

On the surface this was less a vehicle for Rogers's ethical and humanist beliefs than a cultural building such as the Pompidou. But under the skin it offered many opportunities to challenge conventional architectural thinking and to offer solutions to its impasses. Young, Goldschmied and Abbott reconvened around it, shortly to be joined by Mike Davies, who had also worked on

Piano + Rogers,
Centre Pompidou, Paris,
1971–77, aerial view
showing the urban
context and the extent
of the piazza

Above: Centre Pompidou,
activity on the piazza
viewed from the escalator

Opposite: Centre
Pompidou. The varied
and dramatic profile of
the exterior elevations
derives from the expressed
services, aligned here to
the street edge

Overleaf: Centre
Pompidou, the west
face seen across the
busy piazza

Centre Pompidou.
Top: Services on the
rue du Renard, the east
face of the structure.

Bottom: Inside, the
double-height forum
provides a generous
public space.

Pompidou. Among the many other architects who came together on the project were Graham Stirk, Ivan Harbour and Andrew Morris, who are now senior directors of Rogers Stirk Harbour + Partners.

In the late 1970s most of the practice's work had been lightweight industrial buildings on greenfield sites. Lloyd's brought them back to an urban context – but unlike with the Centre Pompidou, the client was a private, commercial organisation. How to make a contribution to the public realm was far less obvious, and took the form of enlivening the immediate context by introducing a series of aesthetic effects such as the depth of light and shadow, intriguing juxtapositions, and unexpected relationships with surroundings like the Victorian Leadenhall Market and Sir Edwin Cooper's 1920s Neoclassical arch.

Another challenge was one Rogers describes as the most difficult of all: how to make meaningful architecture where most of the accommodation is generic office space. Unlike most speculative commercial buildings, Lloyd's had some unique spaces, but it still needed large amounts of ordinary working areas. A series of contemporaneous notes, made in conjunction with a research project for the furniture-makers Knoll and written with an awareness of the imminent IT revolution if not of all its consequences, shows Rogers's grasp of the relationship between spatial and social organisation. 'Hierarchy of uses – spectrum from corporate to individual... cellular to open... intensely/ too loosely controlled.' Most powerful is the concluding remark: 'Sameness + institutional expression must be overcome. There are enormous differences in the character of individuals and organisations and their goals which must be capable of expression.'

How to make meaningful architecture for large buildings with generic interiors remains one of the greatest challenges. Rogers's Leadenhall Building, immediately opposite Lloyd's and under construction at the time of writing, is even bigger than its neighbour and lacks the unique features of the Lloyd's interior. But it manages to conjure a large public plaza at its base, while its design, materials and construction maximise the light within as well as the views out. The goal is to exceed necessity. As Graham Stirk says of the external elevators, 'We turn an uplifting moment into an uplifting experience.' In different ways, from different

Above: Richard Rogers
Partnership, Lloyd's
of London, 1978–86.
The Room in use

Opposite: Lloyd's of
London. The sculptural
expression of the services
energises London's urban
landscape

Overleaf: Lloyd's of
London, detail of the
external services

Richard + Su Rogers,
Dr Rogers's House,
Wimbledon, London,
1968–69. Rogers has
described the house, top,
as 'a transparent tube
with solid boundary walls'.

The interior, bottom,
is furnished eclectically,
including pieces by
Ernesto Rogers

Richard Rogers's parents, Nino and Dada Rogers, 1932 (photographer unknown)

eras and for different briefs, this pair of buildings show appearance – the aesthetic – can be more than just a way of communicating function or slotting unobtrusively into context: it can add to people's experience of the public realm and so improve it.

The inseparability of ethics and aesthetics underlies Rogers's work from the beginning. Even the most striking visual features, from the transparency of his parents' house in Wimbledon designed in 1968–69, to the complex texturing of Leadenhall, have an ethical dimension, and very often one which implies some sort of relationship between occupants and members of the public. Through its appearance, then, architecture becomes a way of structuring space and defining places for a variety of activities, nurturing the complex ecology of social interaction. This core principle, with all the degrees of variation implied by different briefs, sites, technologies and ambitions, is what gives Rogers's work a coherence but also renders it collaborative and invites contributions and participation from many sources. It is, by the same token, what makes it possible for people who are significant talents in their own right, from Young and Abbott to Stirk and Harbour, to flourish in association with each other.

Beyond this is another constant idea in his oeuvre: that architecture provides a frame for human life. It is empowering and fulfilling rather than coercive or hierarchical. Above all, it should offer opportunities for interaction of people with each other, with objects and spaces, with sights, sounds, smells and tastes, and with ideas. This side of his work is strongly apparent in his ideas about public space, but it is also very present in the two homes he has designed for close family, the house for his parents in Wimbledon, and his own house in Chelsea. If in one sense they bear out his belief that family is even more important than architecture, they also demonstrate that his own extended family relationships are an indication of the sociability that architecture can foster. To get something out of life, one has to engage with it – and the quality and attraction of the environment around us can encourage us to do so. Rogers has been issuing the invitation from the beginning of his career and continues to offer it still.

BRIDGE APPROA

'Cities as they could be': Michael Heseltine on Rogers and Regeneration

Jeremy Melvin

Michael Heseltine,
Tony Travers and
Richard Rogers at the
London Conference,
November 2012

Page 40: Richard Rogers
Partnership, Coin Street
development, London,
1979–83, concept sketch
of bridge

The Conservative former Deputy Prime Minister Michael – now Lord – Heseltine has been one of the leading political figures in the revival of British cities since the 1970s. He was a junior minister in the Department of the Environment in the early 1970s, had two stints as Secretary of State in that department in 1979–83 and 1990–92, and continues now as an advisor to government. His report on stimulating economic growth in the regions, 'No Stone Unturned', was largely adopted by the Treasury in 2013.

Heseltine's initiatives provide a political parallel to Richard Rogers's own advocacy of the benefits of a vibrant urban culture. Exact contemporaries, they have contributed much of the scaffolding for the revival of urban life, communities and culture over the last twenty years: the Conservative politician establishing a policy framework and bringing urban concerns to the heart of government; the Labour-supporting architect offering compelling visions in the form of design proposals, theoretical works and, as chair of the Urban Task Force and as advisor to mayors, in policy as well. Though they have never worked together directly, their initiatives have established a field of ambitions and possibilities and paved the way for the working relationships that Rogers forged with the Conservative Secretary of State for the Environment John Gummer, and with John Prescott, who succeeded Heseltine as Deputy Prime Minister when Labour came to power in 1997. Prescott, Rogers points out, was the cabinet minister responsible for the environment as well as Deputy Prime Minister, and it was he who agreed that the headline need for four million new homes in the UK made it urgent to address the decaying state of most British cities, and so paved the way for the 'urban renaissance'.

The contributions of Rogers and Heseltine on the same panel at the London Conference in November 2012 revealed strong affinities in their thinking. Heseltine advocated a massive expansion of his concept for the London Docklands Development Corporation launched in 1979, arguing for a new authority with a remit from the Docks to the East Coast. 'I'd put a driving team of public- and private-sector people in, with Richard Rogers as chairman,' he said on that occasion. Rogers, who as advisor to the Mayor of London galvanised much of the revival of East London, responded, 'I'd do exactly what Michael proposes. East London is where all the potential is, the river is more beautiful, the sea fantastic, there's lots of space and a lot of brownfield land which you can build on. And Michael and I could work together.' Reflecting on the discussion, Heseltine observes, 'Anyone hoping for disagreement would have been bitterly disappointed.'

At the conference Heseltine argued strongly for more 'place-based policy', in contrast to the output of functionally driven central-government departments responsible for issues such as health and education. The UK is unlike most broadly prosperous societies, he pointed out, which have locally developed policies. On becoming Secretary of State for the Environment in 1979, his own response was to continue the initiative of his Labour predecessor Peter Shore, targeting resources at inner-city deprivation, but on condition that the private sector worked with public bodies. The London Docklands Development Corporation, with its remit to bring life back to 2,400 derelict hectares of East London, was one of the first fruits of the policy.

'Place' also plays a central role in Rogers's approach to creating successful urban environments. The Royal Academy of Arts exhibition 'Richard Rogers RA: Inside Out' explores his concept of 'a sense of place': how an intimate awareness of the particular characteristics of a location is a basis for enhancing it. Several seminal projects of the 1980s, such as the Coin Street development on London's South Bank and the polemical proposal for 'London as it could be', exhibited at the Royal Academy in 1986, showed how a sense of place might grow into a vision for large-scale urban improvement and regeneration. But at that time the Greater London Council was being wound up, and the city had no coherent mechanism for developing policy from and around the needs of place.

Working in cities with strong local authorities and decision-making powers encouraged Rogers to agitate for a Mayor of London with control over planning and development. Announced as Labour Party policy by Tony Blair at a 1996 debate organised by the Architecture Foundation, then under Rogers's chairmanship, the post was created in 2000 and Rogers became directly involved in place-based policy-making as head of the Greater London Authority's Architecture and Urbanism Unit.

For both Heseltine and Rogers, the real measure of a successful place is how it contributes to the lives of its inhabitants. In blighted inner-city areas, 'derelict land from which economic

Richard Rogers Partnership, 'London as it could be', 1986. The installation at the Royal Academy of Arts in London included a scheme for restoring Somerset House's relationship to the river through the relocation of the road and the provision of a water garden in its place

Right: 'London as it could be', model and drawing of a lightweight bridge over the River Thames. The installation presented a vision of the metropolis in which the river became a focus for activity rather than a gulf between North and South Banks

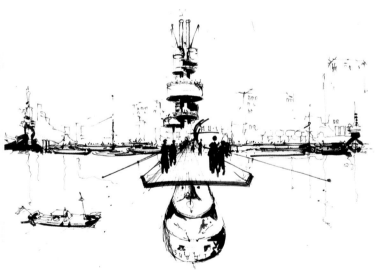

Overleaf: 'London as it could be', sketch for a lightweight bridge over the River Thames

Pages 48–49: 'London as it could be', model. The new bridge and floating islands contained shops, galleries and restaurants

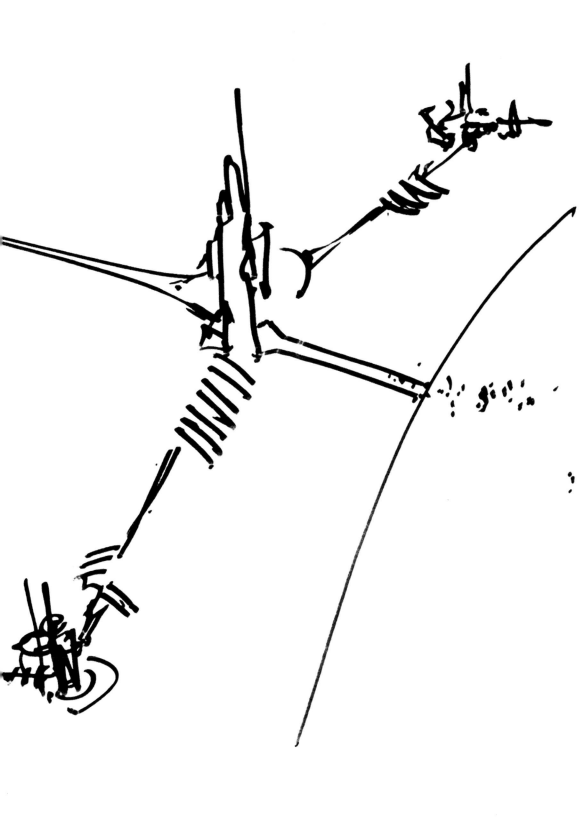

Richard Rogers
Partnership, Greenwich
Peninsula masterplan,
London, 1997–2000,
illustrative drawing

use had gone, leaving behind a skeleton of deprivation,' says Heseltine, 'architecture should be life-enhancing, a light at the end of the tunnel.' He continues, 'An iconic building that attracts interest can itself be a generator though, as Richard and I would agree, architecture is not just about building buildings. It is also about creating a community in the widest sense. But that is not about imposing a plan on people.' Instead, the goal is to create 'conditions that they themselves want, and good-quality housing and good-looking buildings offer a much better chance of success.' In Rogers's terms, they would help to create and enhance a sense of place.

The Greenwich Peninsula is one place where Rogers's and Heseltine's efforts have jointly contributed to regeneration. For Heseltine, it is 'associated with the decision I took in 1979 to launch the London Docklands Development Corporation.' A moment of weakness led him to follow the advice of his officials – offered after 'I had won the political battle' and received their congratulations – 'to leave Greenwich and Lewisham out'. Becoming a member of the Millennium Commission, the body charged with organising a national celebration for the year 2000, provided an opportunity to rectify that omission.

All sorts of uncertainties marked the Commission's efforts, from the impending change of government in the run-up to the 1997 General Election, to disputes over the content and even the site for the celebration. Rogers's Millennium Dome as its centrepiece, though, turned out to be 'a triumph, a brilliant way of creating a large enclosure', and built with 'not a penny of public money'. Despite Heseltine's reservations over its original uses – 'a model of how not to create a great national event' – it has subsequently become 'the most popular entertainment venue in Europe'. Such success comes from 'not being too prescriptive. Richard didn't know he would have an entertainment centre', just as 'I didn't know what would happen on 6,000 acres' of East London handed over to the London Docklands Development Corporation, 'but we knew if we created opportunities exciting things would happen.' Politicians and architects can provide the policy and physical framework for regeneration, but its real goal is such serendipitous fusions of communal desires and opportunities.

Richard Rogers
Partnership, Millennium
Dome, Greenwich,
London, 2000.
Top: The building was
an important element in
the plan to regenerate
the entire Greenwich
peninsula

Bottom: The vast interior
space is column free and
ultimately flexible

Overleaf: Millennium
Dome viewed across the
River Thames at dusk

In Conversation

Michael Craig-Martin and Richard Rogers

Top: Richard Rogers at Yale, 1962. Norman Foster is seated in the centre; Rogers is lying down

Bottom: Michael Craig-Martin under his work 'An Oak Tree', portrait by Jorge Lewinski, 1974

Page 54: Richard + Su Rogers, Dr Rogers's House, Wimbledon, London, 1968–69, concept sketch

Michael Craig-Martin: Richard, you and I come from a similar moment. As students we were steeped in Modernism, and we both happened to be at Yale at the same time in the early 1960s – although I don't think we met.

Richard Rogers: Yes. We didn't suffer from the shock of the new, which was very strong in Britain after the Second World War, especially in the visual arts. Yale was a clear expression of the spirit of Modernism and modernity and it had the greatest teachers of art and architecture.

MCM: I grew up in the United States and by the time I was fourteen, if something was modern it interested me. Yale was the focus of a certain tradition of European Modernism that had migrated to the States, and I wanted to be part of that.

RR: The strongest impact any image has ever had on me was the New York skyline when I arrived by ship. I'd left the three-storey buildings of Southampton, and since there were no tall buildings along Wall Street then, it seemed as if Midtown rose from the sea.

There were significant social problems, of course, like the discrimination against black people. I was horrified when we travelled in the South to find that even at a one-pump filling station there were four toilets and four taps, for men and women, black and white.

But aside from the segregation, to experience America then was visually and socially very impressive.

MCM: We were fortunate to be young at a moment of great optimism, when it seemed possible that we might create a better world. In comparison with Europe, which was still suffering from the effects of the war, the US seemed a beacon of modernity.

RR: John Kennedy was the embodiment of this spirit, a leader of a society eager to move forward with the revolution of the 1960s. Sadly, this started to unravel with his assassination.

MCM: At Yale I had a complete 'Albers education'. Even though Josef Albers had left, his courses were still being taught. He was

Richard and Su Rogers
outside the Embassy
Cinema, New York, 1961

Top: Josef Albers,
*Homage to the Square:
Alone*, 1963. Oil on
canvas, 48 x 48 cm.
Newark Museum,
Newark, NJ

Bottom: Naum Gabo,
*Constructed Head
No. 2*, first version 1916

more interested in the visual than in abstract ideas or context. Was that true in the architecture school too?

RR: Paul Rudolph was much more interested in the visual relationship than the social and functional relationships that predominated in Europe. He always made a model before he put pen to paper; he was quite sculpture-oriented. It was a shock for me. I had had terrific teachers at the Architectural Association in London such as Reyner Banham, Jim Stirling, Alan Colquhoun and Peter Smithson, but they made an intellectual statement and then built from that.

MCM: I have a sense that the visual dominated the arts at that time. It became less true later, and for me it was because of Albers. He had a way of being intelligent visually, a belief that you need to train yourself visually, to practise, to look at something, to unwrap it in a visual way in order to create.

You yourself have an interesting lifetime connection to art and the art world. How did that develop at Yale?

RR: My strongest connections at the time were with Naum Gabo and Alexander Calder. Gabo was a friend of Su [Rogers]'s parents and we lived with him when we were at Yale. But there he was no longer seen as cutting edge and I had difficulty organising a lecture for him. Later, Philip Guston also became a close friend.

MCM: I remember him coming to Yale one day. It was about the time Op Art and Pop Art were emerging, which went against so many ideas that had come to us through Abstract Expressionism. One student said, 'Art is under threat, we should try to defend art from the barbarians.' Guston replied, 'The most dangerous people are those who say they are trying to defend art from the barbarians. Art looks after itself.'

That being said, when I came to Britain in 1966 to teach at Bath Academy of Art I was struck by the level of sophistication and how good it was – it was close to Yale. I was hired to teach straight from graduate school. I sent twelve slides and was offered a job.

RR: That shows somebody was on the ball.

MCM: My colleagues included Tom Phillips and Mark Lancaster, and I met Howard Hodgkin, Richard Smith and Bridget Riley. Remarkably, Claes Oldenburg came to Bath to lecture. But despite all these extraordinary people, there was no 'art world' as there was in America – no galleries, no collectors.

There was a core of people, though – the British Council, the Arts Council and Tate – who were doing amazing things even in the late 1960s. What happened in the 1990s started in the 1950s and 1960s – there was an extraordinary continuity of people in each field.

RR: Back in Britain I was jealous of the theatre, since modern theatre seemed to flourish here more than the other arts. And the National Theatre really was a national institution.

MCM: In Britain the theatre spoke of Modernist ideas. There was a moment in the 1960s and early 1970s when there was quite a bit of slippage between theatre and art, art and architecture, architecture and design. A lot of things became fixed and clear ten years later, but they were not pinned down yet.

RR: At Yale I was very influenced by Vincent Scully. He opened up ways of looking at Henry Hobson Richardson and Louis Sullivan, and also Frank Lloyd Wright, who was directly relevant to me. On a tour of Wright's buildings with Norman Foster we also discovered industrial plants that had the same sort of qualities as great nineteenth-century British railway stations – these powerful images have remained with me.

When I came back to Britain, Team 4 was set up with Su and Norman and Wendy Foster. It took years to absorb their influence and get over Wright's. Creek Vean, a house for my parents-in-law, began to break away, but even now I still keep some sense of the character of a site as a result of Wright's effect on me.

In thinking about how architecture could serve social and political conditions, Creek Vean was a disaster. It took five architects five years to design, when the country needed 300,000 houses a year.

Then Peter Parker, who was not many years older than we were, asked us to design a little factory for Reliance Controls. We thought this project was an opportunity to absorb American lessons, in particular from the Case Study houses, using lightweight steel and fast building methods.

MCM: In the States, the British artists I knew of were sculptors like Anthony Caro and Pop artists like Eduardo Paolozzi. The most contemporary British architecture I knew was Archigram, who were very speculative and very venturesome.

RR: And there's a crossover between them and big industrial plants. I knew Peter Cook of Archigram because he was in my year at the Architectural Association. The group were truly visual and inventive but they were never very interested in the social aspects of architecture. The Futurists, who they sometimes refer to, were political, but they were not. They were idealists rather than political.

This raises a point which fascinates me about how we absorb influences. Archigram influenced Cedric Price and Joan Littlewood in their design for the Fun Palace, but there were other things too. Joan and Cedric also brought left-wing political and social concepts into it, which appeals to me.

I think influence is something you store at the back of your mind which then surfaces at the right time. People have mentioned that the piazza at Beaubourg was influenced by the Piazza del Campo in Siena – I'm sure it was in my mind but we didn't set out to copy it.

I prefer 'Beaubourg' to 'Pompidou' as it refers to the area and stresses that it is less a building than a place.

MCM: That fits with your interest in urban life and the city, its fabric, its public spaces and the way people live in it.

Beaubourg was one of the great moments of European art and culture, an extraordinary thing to happen in Paris.

RR: When we were working on Beaubourg we were certainly not conscious of it being a great moment. I even fought against doing the competition. Being left wing, I didn't like the idea of a centralised cultural institution dominated by and named after the French president.

The design came out of a philosophy of growth and change, separation of structure and services, and clear floors. In this building the plans are not critical, it's the sections that matter. The floor plans are just big pieces of ground. The façade and the piazza are public. The original design for the façade was entirely electronic, learning a little from Piccadilly Circus and a lot from Times Square, and absorbing ideas from both Archigram and Cedric Price.

Calling it a 'place for all people' immediately defines the building as a social catalyst. One thing that was better than we anticipated was the way the French adopted it. The promenade over the building became a natural part of life.

The big breakthrough was having Robert Bordaz, the first president of Beaubourg, as client. He had never built anything but he had been in charge of the French withdrawal from Vietnam and had a great training as a judge. You cannot design a great building without a great client.

MCM: I can hardly think of anything else that sums up a moment so accurately. It is exactly what the moment felt like – socially, politically, in terms of art and of how one might think of the relationship between audiences and art.

You gave the French this machine and they manipulated it and instinctively knew how to make use of it. It seems to me to be a mixture of extreme naivety and extreme sophistication: it's crazy, but that's one reason why it remains such a magical place.

London had to wait until 2000 and the opening of Tate Modern

Herzog & de Meuron,
Tate Modern, London,
1998–2000, Turbine Hall

for a similar moment when the city and the art world came together. Just as Beaubourg transformed the whole of the Marais, so the arrival of a cultural institution transformed Southwark. I was a trustee at the time, and I can remember how nervous we were as we were about to launch Tate Modern. But the doors opened and the public loved it.

RR: It was exactly the same at Beaubourg.

MCM: It was the Turbine Hall that did it for the Tate.

RR: It could have been a disastrous empty space.

MCM: The great thing is to treat it as nothing less than the giant space it is, and something that no one else can provide.

RR: When I was chair of the Tate Trustees in the 1980s it was very bureaucratic. But it suddenly exploded. Private money came into contemporary art; the Saatchis opened up their private world; there was your revolution in education when you made Goldsmiths a great school that really flowered in the 1980s and 1990s; and of course the influence of Nick Serota, whom we appointed to run Tate.

MCM: The art world was elated that such a young man as Nick, in his early forties at the time, had got the right job at the right moment. If the Tate had had anybody other than Nick it would have ended up with another wing at the back of Millbank. The idea of a 100% new museum in a different location on a vast scale transformed the visual arts in the UK.
    Your project for the National Gallery might have been a similar catalyst. You were thinking about Trafalgar Square and how you could transform the city through its public space.

RR: We developed that in 'London as it could be', the experimental project we showed at the Royal Academy in the 1980s. I don't think that any idea is new, but I'm a great believer in taking ideas forward. We took our thinking forward based on what had been done before.

Top: Trafalgar Square, London, after semi-pedestrianisation

Bottom: Richard Rogers Partnership, 'London as it could be', Royal Academy of Arts, London, 1986

MCM: I know we agree that to be a contemporary creative person, and in order to be true to the masters of the past, you have to be of your own time. The least honourable thing is to do a pastiche; that isn't the way they worked.

RR: Everything modern is of its own time. At an inaugural lunch for Lloyds I was the only member of the design team to be invited. I sat next to the Dean of St Paul's, who asked me, 'Are you feeling beleaguered, Mr Rogers?', since I was being slaughtered by the media. He told me a story about Christopher Wren. During the forty years it took Wren to build St Paul's he became so fed up with the ongoing criticism that he built an 18-foot wattle fence around the site to keep out prying eyes. Wren was opposed for being a Modernist of his time.

MCM: Now, thankfully, the general population has embraced so much of what is happening in the visual arts and architecture.
We both have a strong attachment to this city, but what do you think will happen to London in the future?

RR: I've grown to love London. I remember thinking that Paris was so much better, but now I think London is an amazing city.
What will happen in the future? There has been a huge change in the last fifteen to twenty years, when London reversed the downward slide, and ever since there has been an immense upward movement in art and architecture. I hope it won't stop.

MCM: It's extraordinary how the country has absorbed this change. The Britain I came to in 1966 has disappeared almost without a trace. When I go back to New York, it is still the city of my childhood. Britain has been far more radical, although it is often thought of as more conservative.

RR: What has transformed London is the whole city becoming a great meeting place. It's difficult to understand how that could have happened without it absorbing foreigners. There's space for whole waves of immigration, and that is part of the wealth of London.

Translating Spaces: Exploring Rogers's Architectural Language

Nicolai Ouroussoff

Above: Piazza del Campo, Siena

Page 64: Richard Rogers Partnership, UOP (Universal Oil Products) factory, Tadworth, 1969–74, detail of the brightly coloured exterior and interior

Any architect whose values were shaped in the 1960s, and who thinks of themselves as socially committed, would have found the last thirty or so years hard to live through. But this may be especially true for Richard Rogers.

Even before Rogers had begun celebrating the completion of the Centre Pompidou, the building that brought him to fame in the mid-1970s and became a worldwide symbol of popular youth culture, the oil-fuelled prosperity that had driven Europe's progressive social agenda was pretty much over. Then came Margaret Thatcher and Ronald Reagan with their reactionary anti-state agenda, which put a virtual end to the kind of socially minded projects Rogers coveted. Soon, Prince Charles and his Postmodernist hit squads began attacking architects like Rogers for destroying England's urban heritage.

Rogers, of course, has designed his share of luxury towers since the Centre Pompidou years. Yet his architecture has remained tethered to a precise time in cultural history, when a new kind of populism – brash, youthful, enamoured of technology – was supplanting the colourless world of the post-war Welfare State, and he has carried the banner of a certain kind of 1960s idealism ever since. He has never repudiated his leftist values; he continues to believe that technology, properly used, can propel us towards a more egalitarian, civilised society.

What makes him an especially unorthodox figure in the world of architecture is that, as the cultural mainstream seemed to turn against him, Rogers became more politically engaged. He not only spoke out against those who were promoting a cynical and reactionary vision of the city, but also threw himself wholeheartedly into the often tedious work of shaping public policy, lobbying politicians and drafting bulky urban studies for government ministries. In the process he emerged as the *grand seigneur* of the architectural left – Britain's most articulate and effective voice for a sane approach to architecture and urban planning.

Rogers was born in Florence into a cultivated family of doctors and engineers who fled Italy for England on the eve of the Second World War. His cultural reference points have ranged from Siena's Piazza del Campo (a major influence on the plaza of the Centre Pompidou) to Filippo Brunelleschi's pioneering designs for the Duomo in Florence, Joseph Paxton's Crystal Palace in London

Pierre Chareau and
Bernard Bijovet, Maison
de Verre, Paris, 1932

and Pierre Chareau's Maison de Verre in Paris. But like many
British architects who came of age in the 1950s and 1960s, he
was especially drawn to the architecture of post-war Los Angeles,
whose structural lightness and informality seemed to represent
a democratic way of building, free of old-world class prejudices
and the crushing weight of history.

Some of Rogers's first projects look as though they would
fit more comfortably in the Santa Monica Mountains than in
suburban England. In a classic early house he designed for his
parents in Wimbledon, Rogers used 'off-the-shelf' components
that were cheap and easily available, just as Raphael Soriano,
an architect Rogers much admired, had in his 1950 Case Study
House. Both saw their work as a model for mass-produced
housing; the difference was in their approach to technology.
If Soriano's project – the product of a triumphant America where
every home seemed to glisten with new appliances – treated
technology as something matter-of-fact, Rogers's version had
a child-like exuberance that was underscored by its canary-yellow
steel frame.

The most original expression of that vision was the Zip-Up
House, the first project to bring Rogers to international attention.
He conceived the house as a prototype for mass-produced
affordable housing, designing a one-storey rectangular yellow
tube raised on bright pink steel columns whose heights could

be adjusted to suit different kinds of terrain, from a flat urban lot to a suburban hillside. The tube was divided into 4-foot-wide (c. 1.2-metre-wide) modular sections: if an owner wanted to expand it, he or she could simply order additional sections, which would then be delivered by truck and installed at the site.

Conceptually, the design owed something to the Soviet Disurbanists, who in the 1920s imagined sombre settlements of individual dwelling units that could be moved around to suit the changing needs of a community. (Several units could be joined together when a couple married and had children, let's say – or pulled apart if they divorced.) But Rogers's design was also a take on the more raucous youth-driven culture of the 1960s, albeit drawing its inspiration from the prosaic world of buses and auto-repair shops rather than the sexily contoured bodies of Jaguars and Triumphs. The Zip-Up House's body was made of the same aluminum panels used to insulate refrigerated trucks, its softly rounded corner windows were taken from double-decker Routemaster buses and its adjustable steel columns were a reference to car jacks.

Over the next few years Rogers strove to translate his vision into socially ambitious works. A portable hospital designed in 1971 for the Association of Rural Aid in Medicine could, in theory, be packed in shipping containers and airlifted to derelict inner-city neighbourhoods or peasant villages in the developing world as a kind of community centre and emergency-care unit. Two years later he and Renzo Piano reworked the Zip-Up prototype for a factory in Surrey.

It's only with the Centre Pompidou, however, designed with Piano, that Rogers's aesthetic values and social ideals fused into a mature style. The project, launched in the wake of the 1968 student uprisings and sited in a seedy working-class Paris neighbourhood frequented by truck drivers and prostitutes, was politically charged. When it was announced that two shaggy-haired foreigners – from London, where Piano was temporarily resident, no less – had won the competition, Parisians were outraged. (Giscard d'Estaing, who succeeded Georges Pompidou as President, reportedly hated the design and ordered one of its most provocative features, the media wall, to be removed because he worried it could become a powerful propaganda tool in the hands of leftist opponents.)

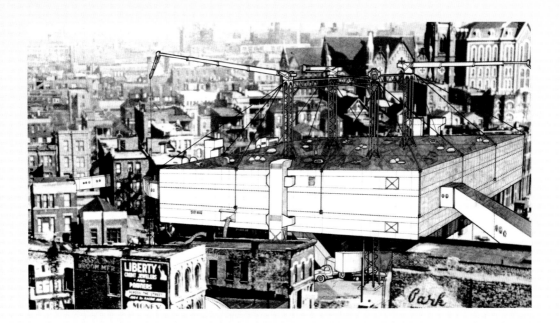

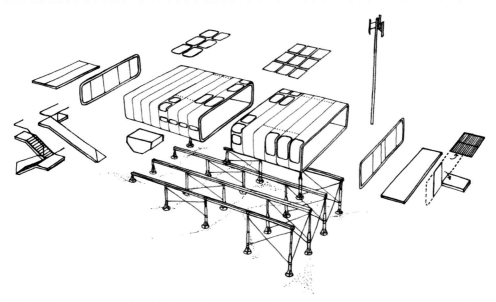

Top: Piano + Rogers,
ARAM module, 1971. The
concept was adaptable to
many contexts, including
deprived urban areas

Bottom: Richard +
Su Rogers, Zip-Up
Enclosures, 1968,
exploded axonometric

Overleaf: Richard +
Su Rogers, Zip-Up
Enclosures. The Zip-
Up House could be
assembled anywhere:
adjustable jacks freed
it from the tyranny of
the site's contours

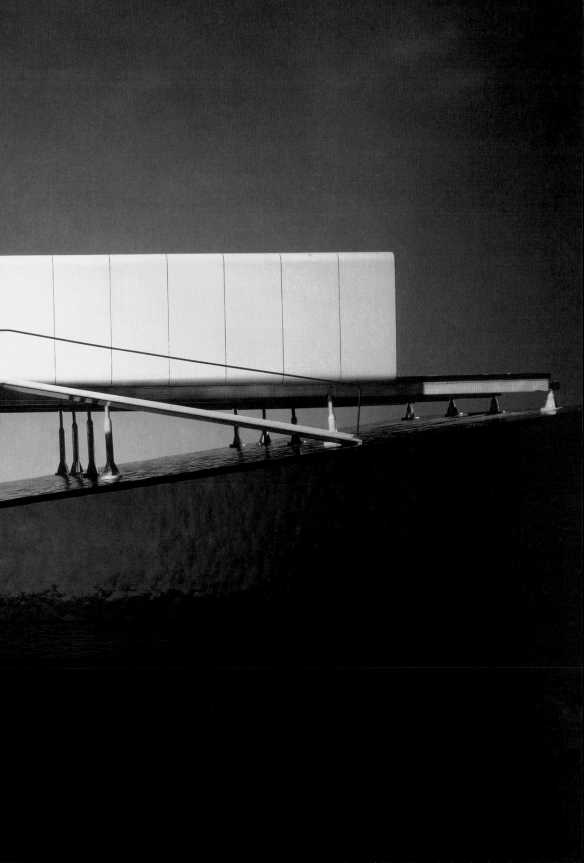

Top: Piano + Rogers,
Centre Pompidou, Paris,
1971–77, view within
the context of the city

Bottom: Richard Rogers
Partnership, Lloyd's of
London, detail of the
external services

The intensity of the reaction was striking given how long similar ideas had been floating in architecture circles – Cedric Price and the radical theatre director Joan Littlewood, for instance, had been pushing their proposal for a populist Fun Palace around London for nearly a decade by then. Yet part of the magic of the Centre Pompidou is the way it was able to capture the mood and ideals of its time. The scaffolding-like main façade, with its tubular glass escalators and over-scaled steel components, was a knock against the often patronising tone of high culture and those who promoted it. The colourful network of structural members, air ducts and water pipes that run up the back of the building expressed the team's desire to create an architectural language that was populist in spirit and could be easily 'read' by a mass audience.

Most important, Rogers and Piano were able to do with the building what they sought to express in its language. On an average day, the centre's main plaza, which is paved with the same type of cobblestones that students hurled at police in '68 – spills over with youthful energy, which flows right into the massive entry hall, up across the façade and into the galleries. And whether or not you buy into the notion that the interiors – whose moveable walls and floors were intended to encourage a fluid and informal relationship between the centre's various departments – have led to the creation of new cultural models, as intended, they certainly make for remarkable public theatre.

Rogers achieved a similar triumph several years later in his design for the Lloyd's of London insurance market, albeit in slightly darker tones. Like the Centre Pompidou, the building looks as if it has been turned inside out, with pipes, air ducts, stairs and elevators extending the height of the exterior. Stainless-steel boxes that house the bathroom units are plugged into one side; bright blue mechanical gantries hang over the edge of the roof to support mechanical window-washing platforms.

The plan freed up interior space, allowing Rogers to create big open floorplates, which he arranged around a central atrium. In a reflection of his obsession with flexibility, the building was designed with three times the necessary office space. Lloyd's initially occupied the four lower floors, which opened on to the atrium and were connected by big escalators to maximise interaction between the traders. Upper floors, which were rented out, were separated from the main atrium by glass windows to provide more privacy. If Lloyd's needed to expand, it could take over some of the upper floors, hoisting in more escalators and removing the glass so the new floors could be integrated with its existing space.

The result was something like a late twentieth-century interpretation of a Gothic cathedral. Lloyd's is more brooding than the Centre Pompidou, the play of light and shadow on its surfaces more extreme. On a sunny day, light cascades down through a barrel-vaulted glass roof into its soaring atrium. Exterior windows on the office floors, by contrast, are made of translucent glass, which gives the lower levels a dreamy subaqueous atmosphere and focuses attention back towards the interior.

But the design was also a knowing commentary on Postmodernist parodies of Classicism, which were then spreading through architecture like a cancer. To Rogers, Postmodernism's arcane references to outdated period styles smacked of snobbery. His own building didn't ignore history: it drew on another lineage – one that was rooted in the industrial age rather than feudal traditions and that extended back through the Japanese Metabolists of the 1960s to Frank Lloyd Wright's Larkin Building of 1904 and the Crystal Palace from the 1850s. At the same time, like the Centre Pompidou, it didn't demand architectural expertise to be understood. Its structural and mechanical systems were expressed with a boldness and clarity that made them accessible to an average person.

By the time of the completion of Lloyd's in 1986, of course, that manner of thinking seemed to have run its course. The age of prosperity that had begun during Rogers's youth – and that had been fuelled by a seemingly endless supply of cheap oil – had come to a crashing halt with the 1973 Yom Kippur War and the Arab oil embargo. By the mid-1980s Thatcherism and Reaganism had hit full stride and the youth culture epitomised by the student riots and anti-war protests of the late 1960s was a dim memory. What's more, architecture itself had abandoned many of its central goals, among them the promise that it could be an active agent of social reform.

For those architects who saw Postmodernism as a reactionary movement, one that was pathologically attached to a pre-industrial world, one way forward was to invent an architecture that was capable of expressing the conflicts, frictions and disharmonies that have riven society while trying to encourage a more open – and promiscuous – vision of social exchange. Rogers took another tack. Refusing to turn his back on his earlier ideals, he began trying to influence public policy more directly.

One of his first salvos was aimed at Prince Charles, who had not only embarked on a very public campaign against modern architecture, but was promoting himself as a spokesperson for the common man, whom he claimed shared his traditional tastes. (Rogers has lost at least two major commissions through the Prince's opposition, most recently a housing project on the site of the former Chelsea Barracks.) In a memorable article published in *The Times* in 1989, Rogers assailed the Prince for blaming architects for most of the city's social ills, asserting that the quality of an urban environment reflects the values of civic and business leaders as much as the talents of architects. Creating parodies of history by adding Classical veneers to modern buildings, he pointed out, wasn't the solution.

It was an unusually strong public statement for an architect – most of whom, as we know, tend to recoil from politics in fear of offending potential clients. And it sparked Rogers to more action. In the run-up to the 1997 General Election, Rogers, who was then chair of the Architecture Foundation, organised a series of well-attended public debates in London, sponsored by the *Evening Standard*, that focused attention on issues such as urban congestion and the shrinking stock of public housing. (Among the solutions discussed were the pedestrianisation of Trafalgar Square and banning cars from the city centre.)

Not long afterwards, Tony Blair, the new Prime Minister, invited Rogers and Deputy Prime Minister John Prescott to set up an Urban Task Force to explore many of these issues in greater depth. Almost all their proposals, including limiting all new developments to brownfield sites and linking them to public transportation, were eventually adopted by Parliament and implemented by London's mayor, Ken Livingstone, with Rogers's guidance.

As the years wore on, Rogers's architecture, too, began to change in subtle ways. Many of his residential and office towers, while still using his trademark brightly coloured exposed-steel structure, were more muted – even polite by the old standards.

Other projects, especially in the civic realm, seemed to shed some of the broodiness of buildings like Lloyd's and become looser and more playful – a response, perhaps, to the formal possibilities created by new computer technologies.

In a design for the Bordeaux Law Courts, one of his most buoyant and theatrical works, seven cone-shaped courtrooms are lined up inside a block of crystalline glass. A narrow bridge leads over a reflecting pool and into the main glass hall, reinforcing the building's formal grandeur. Inside, more bridges cross overhead, alerting you to the everyday movements of lawyers, judges, plaintiffs, defendants and clerks – the law, with all of its hierarchies, in action. Inside the courtrooms, a beam of heavenly light filters down through a central oculus, as if to reinforce the authority and wisdom of the court. It's a project that celebrates the nobility of law, its central role in a democratic society.

Similarly, the Terminal 4 building at Madrid's Barajas Airport – one of the most spectacular terminals built in years – reasserts a tradition that extends back in spirit through the glamour years of air travel to the great nineteenth-century railway stations. A roof of undulating steel is supported on big Y-shaped yellow columns that rise up between the concrete walkways – some as wide as runways – leading to the gates. In the loveliest of the spaces, you can peer down three floors to the train and metro stations – a trenchant symbol for a mobile society.

Rogers has been fighting so long, in fact, that the historical tide he first battled against so many years ago may finally be turning his way. No sane architect talks about a return to Classicism any more. Prince Charles has been pushed out of the headlines by his two sons, who seem to have a very different range of interests. And the drive towards privatisation that has been nibbling away at the public realm – and that has corrupted so much of the architecture of the past decade – may finally be showing a few signs of waning. If so, it would have a profound effect on how our public spaces are shaped and designed. Rogers may one day be recognised as a figure who carried the populist torch through a long period of darkness.

Bordeaux Law Courts.
The offices are linked
to the individual courts
by glass bridges across
a central canyon

Richard Rogers
Partnership, Terminal 4,
Madrid Barajas Airport,
1997–2005, road
entrance

Opposite: Terminal 4,
Madrid Barajas Airport.
A finely graduated
spectrum of colour
draws attention to the
dynamic structure

Overleaf: Terminal 4,
Madrid Barajas Airport,
skylit interior

Cities and Civic Responsibility

Anne Power

Anne Power

Page 84: Richard Rogers Partnership, Shanghai Redevelopment, model to show massing of buildings. The masterplan was designed as a mixed-use development with offices and shops concentrated around underground stations

I first learned about Richard Rogers's commitment to social inclusion when we visited the Isle of Dogs in East London in 1987. I took him round five nearby council estates that were currently standing in the way of powerful developers. Richard wanted to understand why these estates seemed so troubled and had such bad reputations – and why they mattered. He immediately warmed to their simple design, their dense vitality, and to the people who lived and worked there. 'There's nothing wrong with the architecture,' was one of his responses. Our tour included the famous Robin Hood Gardens housing complex in Poplar, designed by Alison and Peter Smithson in the late 1960s but threatened by demolition to make way for expensive new developments. Richard and I have since argued for its preservation as valuable and attractive to the local community.

Inspired by these visits, Richard then wanted to see the Broadwater Farm estate in Tottenham, north London, where the Priority Estates Project, a not-for-profit consultancy, was helping the community and council to secure a long-term solution to social unrest. Two years earlier, Cynthia Jarrett, mother of a young man arrested and charged with various offences, had died following a police raid. This led to serious rioting by young people on the estate and the murder of a popular local policeman, PC Keith Blakelock. Richard met the estate's youth association leaders, watched enterprise workshops in action, walked with caretakers and community organisers on their patrols. He saw the residents' plans for a Peace Garden to commemorate PC Blakelock and Cynthia Jarrett. He was deeply impressed by the energy and vitality of the young black residents and their potential for community self-help. His immediate response was, 'If this can happen here, it can happen everywhere.' That's why we set out together to establish a national support and training organisation for people living and working in similar areas.

The visits to Broadwater Farm and the Isle of Dogs inspired Richard's passionate and lasting commitment to training communities in how to manage and improve local conditions – based on the work he saw the Priority Estates Project carry out in Tottenham. He felt it was crucial to give this commitment a national focus, and this led to the founding in 1991 of the National Communities Resource Centre, a charity he chaired for twelve years and which is now based at Trafford Hall, Chester. One of our

Self-build houses at Trafford Hall accommodate people attending courses and demonstrate a possible option for residents of deprived areas to improve their own lives

initiatives was a series of self-build houses. Its creation involved working with and winning over, among others, the Conservative government, Prince Charles, Martin and Christopher Laing (of the construction company John Laing), Sir Allen Sheppard of Grand Metropolitan, John Riddell, David Sainsbury, and multiple tenants' organisations and community groups. The Centre opened in 1995 and to date it has delivered training and small pump-priming grants to help more than 100,000 people.

Richard cares passionately about cities and the communities they house – their potential for beauty or ugliness, for social integration or divisiveness, their environmental potential or impact. Negotiating this tug-of-war employs all his creative, artistic and social skills. Harsh as his criticisms of the UK might sometimes seem – especially in contrast to his love affair with Barcelona – during the 1990s his arguments prevailed. His influence on John Gummer, Conservative Secretary of State for the Environment from 1993 to 1997, led to a ban on the construction of out-of-town shopping centres and a requirement to build within rather than outside cities. Britain's cities, which were in a shocking state of decay in the 1980s compared with those of France, Italy or Spain, began a journey of recovery. You could almost argue that Richard's extraordinary architecture was like a counterpoint to the theme tune of vibrant social life and vitality in busy, loved cities.

It was Barcelona, the decayed, declining, soot-blackened, industrially fouled Mediterranean port of past glory, that became Richard's Mecca. The strongly emerging local democracy of post-Franco Spain impelled recovery. The city's careful layout, dense street patterns and enclosed courtyards, the joy of strolling along pavements lined with small shops, craft centres and cafés, the curiously ornamental, semi-vernacular architecture of the Catalan Antoni Gaudí and the mix of local pride and extrovert internationalism all contributed to Barcelona's winning bid for the Olympic Games of 1992. Richard became architectural advisor to the city, enthralled by the Catalan instinct for social life. He praises Barcelona's small squares and courtyards, reclaimed in a prelude to the Olympic bid as monuments to citizen involvement and self-help. (Not for nothing is Joan Clos, Mayor of Barcelona at the time of Richard's involvement, now the head of UN-Habitat in Nairobi.) Barcelona is hitting harder times today, but it still

Barcelona, aerial views
showing the waterfront,
bottom, and city grid
established by Ildefons
Cerdà in the mid-
nineteenth century, top

acts as a social and physical magnet attracting young people from across the world and has a vitality that will carry it through.

Back in the UK, the landslide victory for progressive, pro-city, pro-social policies heralded by the Labour General Election win of 1997 was music to Richard's ears and in part influenced by him. His Reith Lectures of 1995 had paved the way. John Prescott, the imposing, straight-speaking Northern seaman who became MP for Hull and Deputy Prime Minister, bought into Richard's vision of compact cities with mixed uses, mixed incomes, tamed traffic and vibrant street life. Prescott invited Richard, by then knighted and a peer, to chair the Urban Task Force, a group of twelve government-appointed city specialists with a remit to find a way forward for Britain's decayed and neglected cities.

Five core challenges reasserted themselves during a year of international site visits, research and debates. The more cities spread out into land-hungry, car-based, affluent suburbs, the more damaged they become. The sheer volume of traffic such cities generate breaks up neighbourhoods and turns central squares into parking lots and roundabouts, imposing uncounted costs on the urban economy. Highly urbanised societies like the UK have become deeply unequal and divided, threatening our entire social fabric. As the industrial power of Europe has declined, so social and economic problems have intensified, leaving a legacy of wasteland, idle infrastructure and dislocated communities. All these problems are encapsulated in the untold environmental harm our former industrial cities caused, placing a huge burden on present-day communities. Without new forms of city government, visionary ideas and clear strategies, the way forward is uncertain.

Five clear messages emerged from Richard's work in the Urban Task Force. We live in a crowded island and continent where land is scarce. It must be protected for the sake of future generations and the natural environment, on which all human life depends. So cities must contain sprawl into greenfield sites and have dense, lively, compact inner areas.

Road traffic is polluting and noisy, eating away at the social and economic vitality of cities, yet transport and mobility are also their lifeblood. More public transport and more integrated planning for cycling and walking – following the example of the best European cities – can transform urban spaces.

Large parts of the labour market, particularly young people,

Richard Rogers
Partnership, 'London as
it could be', images of
Trafalgar Square from
the 'Foster Rogers Stirling'
exhibition at the Royal
Academy of Arts
in London, 1986.

Top: the square choked
by traffic before its semi-
pedestrianisation; bottom:
opening up a terrace
in front of the National
Gallery allowed free
pedestrian movement
and a sculpture garden

are currently excluded from work; poor communities are marginalised while grotesque levels of over-consumption by the rich undermine our social structures. We need to rethink our approach to social and economic problems, to generate a virtuous circle of jobs, access to training and know-how, enterprise and innovation.

New leadership can reverse urban decay and generate new ideas. Barcelona, London, Turin and Lille have all recovered strongly following the election of visionary and people-oriented mayors. However, other layers of governance must also be in place, above all structures encouraging and enabling citizen participation. The best-led cities disaggregate plans and execution down to community level and empower citizens to take on new community roles.

The fifth, and possibly most important theme, is the natural environment on which city survival depends. Cities concentrate people in small spaces, thereby potentially saving energy, land and materials. However, they are also hugely wasteful, constantly destroying what is already there to create anew and devouring scarce resources with scant regard for the consequences. How do we conserve, share, protect, renew and reinvest in urban patterns that are more people- and planet-friendly?

Richard and I wrote the five key messages of the Urban Task Force into *Cities for a Small Country* (2000), arguing that a well governed, traffic-tamed, socially integrated, innovation-oriented city economy can shape a better future for our planet – more sustainable, fairer, more attractive. Richard expounded on the power of design to create beautiful places, working out ways to combine his social sensitivity and passion for justice with his aesthetic and humanist commitment to urban design. My community experience provided the glue for our shared belief that when given the chance people can develop their own problem-solving skills; in multiple small ways, they can make the world a better place.

Legacies of an Archaic Modernist: Embracing Cities, Shaping London

Ricky Burdett

Page 92: Richard Rogers
reading and working
in Tuscany

The archaic Modernist

Beneath the gnarled branches and robust trunk of a century-old
Tuscan oak (*Quercus frainetto*) in the Val d'Orcia, Richard Rogers
is already at work at six in the morning. Bent over his leather hold-
all, flipping through piles of plastic folders marked up with DayGlo
pink and yellow Post-it notes, he starts his day early – wherever
he is. His angular frame invariably clad in vibrant colours, he
moves deliberately as he consults his pink rubber-clad iPhone
or scribbles down thoughts with his signature green felt pen.
The arch-Modern architect and urbanist, author of some of the
most radical buildings of the last 40 years, is totally at home
in this ancient landscape.

Born 80 years ago in Florence, less than an hour's drive from
the Val d'Orcia, Rogers displays an attachment to this land that
is both visceral and contemporary. His life has been a balancing
act between past and future, between Italian cultural values and
progressive English pragmatism, between designing responsive
buildings and raising awareness about the health of the planet.
These contrasts have endowed him with a deeply humanist
and positivist outlook: a strong political ethos that has shaped
his practice and thinking in architecture and city-making over
the last five decades.

As the author of buildings and projects in megacities around
the world, from Shanghai to Mexico City, it is difficult to imagine
that for Rogers small Tuscan towns have been a continuing source
of inspiration. Standing in the main square of Pienza in his cobalt
blue shirt, he blends into an environment infused with the hues
and shades of frescoes by Giotto or Piero della Francesca, or works
by the early masters of the Quattrocento who gave birth to the
Renaissance in towns and villages nearby.

In the near-perfect urban artefact of Pienza, Rogers enthuses
about the fifteenth-century architect Bernardo Rossellino and his
client, the great patron Pope Pius II. Together they created one
of the most beautiful set pieces of any city in the world. It is not
only the shape, scale and texture of the buildings and spaces that
appeal to Rogers – from the worn marble public seating at the base
of the Bishop's Palace to the exquisite detailing of the 500-year-
old paving – but also the perfect harmony between city and nature,
which represents, in his eyes, a synthesis of the environmental
and social potential of architectural and urban form.

Rogers often surprises audiences in Asia or the Americas (where cities of twenty million sprawl endlessly towards the horizon) with picture-postcard views of such elemental, 'compact' cities, perched on the tops of hills and enclosed by walls that stop abruptly as the Tuscan countryside begins. The lessons to be learned, for him, are clear. However large or small, regardless of geographical location and economic power, cities are delicate eco-systems that can be 'designed' to be sustainable, or not. As with Rossellino and Pope Pius II, it is the role of the architect and his or her patron – whether mayor or minister, developer or investor – to understand architecture as a spatial and ethical art with profound social and environmental consequences. It is this mission, pursued relentlessly and passionately for decades, that has kept Richard Rogers at the foreground of public debate in both the UK and abroad.

Embracing cities

More than any designer in the post-Second World War era, Richard Rogers has made cities the focus of attention and placed the environment and society on the architectural agenda. In this he follows in the tradition of the great urban proselytisers Ebenezer Howard, Lewis Mumford and Jane Jacobs, but with far more edge. He has the urgency of a practising architect with a deep belief in the transformative power of design and technology.

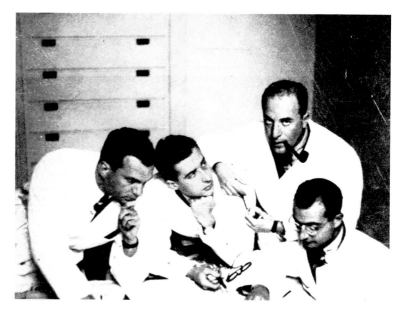

In this he has been strongly influenced by the ethical perspective
of his elder cousin Ernesto Nathan Rogers, one of the major
intellectuals and architectural critics and practitioners (with
BBPR and as editor of *Casabella*) of mid-twentieth-century Italy.

At a time when Modernism was regarded as a social failure and
design had become increasingly aestheticised, Richard Rogers
worked hard to re-socialise architectural and urban practice.
It is easy to forget how abstract the architectural debate had
become by the 1970s and 1980s, when style and form shaped
both discourse and practice. Postmodernism, Neoclassicism,
Late-Modernism and High-Tech (a term Rogers has always
shunned) were the keywords of the architectural elites of the
day. The decline of post-1945 state interventionism and the
establishment of neo-liberalism in the UK and US relegated
architecture to a de-socialised practice, with cities seen as the
province of technical planners and bureaucrats.

Rogers's humanist outlook and uncompromising belief in the
power of design (new technologies, new materials, new forms
of communication) have allowed him to carve out a unique place
among twentieth- and early twenty-first-century architects.
Le Corbusier, Frank Lloyd Wright, Mies van der Rohe, Frank
Gehry, Norman Foster, Rem Koolhaas and Zaha Hadid have

all played a fundamental role in reshaping the debate and language of architecture, but Rogers stands alone in working within the profession and on the edges, at the interface between design and the political. His office always comes top among the most desirable architectural practices for young designers to work in and he is regularly asked by 10 Downing Street to consult on urban policy.

Rogers's combination of die-hard optimism, natural communication skills, unshakable self-assuredness and prize-fighter tenacity is a powerful cocktail that has worked effectively across different constituencies of clients, politicians, fellow designers and cultural commentators. As critic and teacher Robert Maxwell has noted, Rogers is a full-bodied Modernist rather than a Revisionist who 'is old enough to be immersed in Modernism, but young enough to have inherited the mantle of Modernism rather than to have invented it.' For Maxwell, Rogers has embraced 'the purpose of avant-garde art which is to change consciousness and prepare for the future.' (*Casabella*, April 1984, pp. 16–71.)

In this respect Rogers has shown himself to be constructively relentless, in his belief both that he is right and that something can be done to improve things. On the popular BBC Radio 4 programme *Desert Island Discs* he acknowledged that he learned this can-do attitude from his enlightened Italian parents, who always supported him as a child after the family arrived in the frosty environment of wartime Britain. Despite bullying at school and rough treatment from his teachers in the face of his dyslexia and the social awkwardness of a foreign child, he claimed that he 'never knew the word impossible'. From this psychological perspective Rogers has developed an ethical and practical philosophy that embraces the future, convinced that 'we have to use technology, politics and art to make our cities liveable for the twenty-first century. The remarkable capacity of technology puts the future on our side.'

Rogers has always been passionate about cities. For him, they are 'the cradle of civilisation, a place for societies to come together and exchange ideas.' Yet when given the chance to contribute to the prestigious BBC Reith Lectures in 1995 (the only practising architect ever to have done so), he used his platform as a rallying cry to do something, to 'stop the rot', to turn cities (like London) round and make them more sustainable as social and environmental metabolisms.

In the mid-1990s Britain was coming out of a deep recession and the political mood was shifting after more than fifteen years of Conservative government. The collapse of the Berlin Wall, the impact of globalisation on national economies and increased awareness of the environmental crisis created a new context for high-level debate. Rogers grasped the opportunity to put cities and sustainability at the heart of the public agenda.

The opening paragraphs of his Reith Lectures give a flavour of his approach: 'Above us, as I speak, the 400 or so satellites currently in orbit witness and gauge the global impact of a human population that has leapt from 1.5 to 5.5 billion in this century alone. Coldly they confirm the grim realities we all experience in our daily lives as we step out into the city. It is a shocking revelation – especially to me as an architect – that the world's environmental crisis is being driven by our cities. For the first time in history, half the world's population live in cities. In 1900 it was only one-tenth. In 30 years, it may be as much as three-quarters. The urban population of the world is increasing at a rate of a quarter of a million people per day – think of it as a new London every month.'

As this extract reveals, Rogers is both an eloquent communicator and a strong advocate of facts and statistics. An avid reader of everything from government reports on housing standards to the latest data on carbon emissions, he works more like a forensic scientist than an artist. He is careful to base his arguments not on subjective impressions but on robust evidence and logic.

Shaping London

Despite working in cities across the globe and having built the canonical late twentieth-century architectural icon in Paris (the Centre Pompidou), it is in London that Rogers has left his greatest mark. But it has not been easy. London is a city that inspires affection and frustration in equal measure. For Rogers, it epitomises the humanist city where his parents chose to live after escaping the tyrannies of Italian Fascism in the 1930s. It is a generous and balanced city where parks, squares and terraces create a high-quality public realm. Yet it is a city that for many years turned its back on the qualities of social equality and public

Richard Rogers
Partnership, Paternoster
Square competition, 1987.
The model, left, describes
the morphology of the
scheme with buildings cut
through by public routes;
the drawing, above, shows
the glazed lower piazza
level with the entrance to
the Underground station

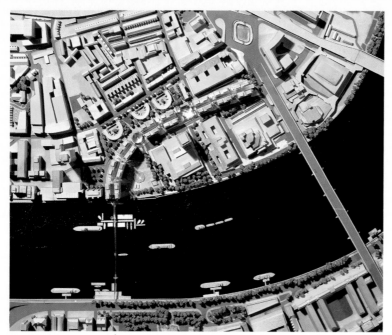

Richard Rogers
Partnership, Coin Street
development, London,
1979–83. The scheme for
a mixed-use development
included a significant
public space on the South
Bank of the River Thames

Opposite: Coin Street
development. Office
provision was broken
down into a series of
towers, leaving the
ground-level space
almost entirely public

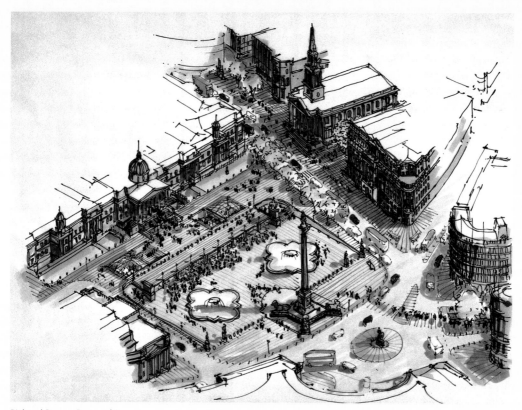

Richard Rogers Partnership,
'London as it could be',
1986, drawing showing
Trafalgar Square reclaimed
for pedestrians

spirit. Many districts degenerated during the 1970s and 1980s; major public spaces were turned into traffic roundabouts and market-led development threatened the delicate social cohesion of the world's first megacity.

Rogers has cared passionately about London since he returned from Paris in the late 1970s. But nearly all his early projects, with the exception of Lloyd's of London, came to nothing. The city became a laboratory of urban ideas for Rogers and his colleagues. His schemes from the early 1980s for the redevelopment of Coin Street on London's South Bank were the first to suggest a new pedestrian crossing for the River Thames. The controversial National Gallery competition of 1982, in which Rogers envisaged opening up Trafalgar Square, stoked a useless debate on architectural style that lasted at least a decade. In 1987, Rogers's imaginative response to the redevelopment of Paternoster Square next to St Paul's Cathedral was ultimately scuppered by princely dark powers. And in the middle of this, at the height of her reign, Margaret Thatcher abolished the Greater London Council (for Rogers, 'a purely vindictive and politically motivated action'), leaving the city without a voice, its future determined by Whitehall civil servants and competing boroughs.

But during this relatively fallow period, in which Rogers considered moving full time to academia as head of the Bartlett School of Architecture at UCL, a number of personal and strategic alliances developed that gave him a unique platform as a tireless campaigner for London. He became a trustee and then chair of the Tate Gallery, a prestigious though then fusty institution that introduced him to new layers of London's political establishment. He was awarded the Royal Gold Medal for architecture in 1985. Significantly, the Royal Academy afforded him his greatest public opportunity in the 1986 'Foster Rogers Stirling' exhibition, where he chose to imagine 'London as it could be'. This memorable installation of fresh ideas for central London and the River Thames contained the seeds of many of the more ambitious projects that have since been realised, though a few remain obstinately still-born.

Some of these ideas and much of the underpinning analysis found their way into *A New London*, a small book written in 1992 with the Labour Shadow Arts Minister Mark Fisher which consolidated Rogers's relationship with New Labour. Despite this, it is a sign of Rogers's authority and relentless campaigning skills that he received many of his most prestigious accolades under Tory governments. He was awarded the Royal Gold Medal and made chair of the Tate Gallery under Margaret Thatcher; he was knighted, later made a member of the House of Lords (as a Labour peer) and invited to give the BBC Reith Lectures under John Major. Only in 1997 was he offered a full role in the New Labour government as chair of the Urban Task Force, which, as Anne Power has described, became instrumental in changing urban policy in England in favour of cities and their regeneration.

In the 1995 Reith Lectures Rogers listed a number of projects and initiatives that could transform the quality of life for London's citizens. He argued for a system of road pricing that would reduce traffic by 30%. Less than a decade later Mayor Ken Livingstone implemented the Congestion Charge, still regarded as a model of good urban governance. Rogers campaigned for the pedestrianisation of Trafalgar Square, linking the National Gallery to the square and its fountains for the enjoyment of all. This was realised by Norman Foster in 2000. In the same radio broadcast, Rogers suggested that Exhibition Road in South Kensington could become a 'pedestrianised millennium avenue, part of a network of tree-lined routes across London'. Dixon Jones completed a version of this project in 2011 in time for the Olympic Games. Rogers argued for the revitalisation of the Thames, especially between Westminster Bridge and Tower Bridge, to make more of London's most 'under-used public amenity'. With the completion of the Millennium Bridge and the opening of Tate Modern this stretch of river has indeed become an active and much used place for visitors and Londoners alike; on summer weekends it is enjoyed by as many as 200,000 people a day.

But Rogers's most profound anxiety for London was political rather than architectural. 'London must not be abandoned to the mercy of the market – to cars, pollution and poverty,' he argued. 'London offers every opportunity to create a cultured, balanced and sustainable city. But to achieve this, Londoners themselves must be empowered to shape their future.' The combined effect of Rogers's advocacy, reinforced by the Architecture Foundation (which he chaired from 1991) and its Public Forum Debates, the changing political mood in the city and the election of the

New Labour government in 1997 led to Londoners being able to vote – for the first time in history – for their own directly elected mayor.

In 2000 Ken Livingstone was voted in as mayor and Rogers was appointed as Chief Advisor on Architecture and Urbanism, offering him the opportunity to push to implement the ideas he had been promoting for decades. It was not a totally smooth ride, with Rogers becoming impatient with political timescales and the debilitating impact of bureaucracy across all government agencies. He worked unpaid with Ken Livingstone for eight years and then stood down after a few bumpy years with Livingstone's successor, Boris Johnson.

Today you can see Rogers's influence throughout the London Plan, the capital's blueprint for future development. It bears the hallmarks of his urban thinking, as it was articulated during previous decades and enshrined in the Urban Task Force report *Towards an Urban Renaissance* (1999). The Green Belt should be protected. Brownfield sites should be developed with new housing and mixed communities. Public transport should be

Richard and Ruth Rogers
at St Leonard's Terrace,
London, portrait by
Richard Bryant

enhanced. The car should be tamed and priority given to cyclists and pedestrians. The public realm should be given a facelift. And, as we have seen with the development that accompanied the 2012 London Olympics, East London should become the focus for sustained investment to make the capital more equitable and sustainable than ever before.

Rogers continues to advocate and agitate for London. Over twenty years ago on *Desert Island Discs* he called for the fences around the city's beautiful squares to be pulled down so all Londoners could enjoy the attractive landscaped spaces that are still reserved for the privileged few. He has returned to this campaign as well as rekindling the debate about the future of Victoria Embankment, the only south-facing stretch of the Thames that remains unfriendly and dominated by the car. He is also raising awareness of the acute housing shortage that is pricing people out of this quintessentially humanist city.

Rogers's affair with London is ongoing and the passion continues to run. An improved, more liveable capital city will be one of his lasting legacies. Few architects, even with a 50-year portfolio, could make such claims for any city, let alone London. Yet Rogers has also left his mark on the urban landscape of other places around the globe and more importantly on the way we think about and design the next generation of cities for an increasingly urban world.

River Café,
Hammersmith

Quercus

Exceptional staying power and an unshakable belief in the art of the possible are Rogers's defining characteristics. As witnessed by the bright collarless shirts and comfortable shoes he has worn for decades, he sticks to his guns and is profoundly loyal. His relationship with an extremely extended family network – sons, daughters-in-law, grandchildren, brother, cousins, in-laws, former partners, office colleagues and hundreds of friends who are considered and consider themselves as family – is as genuine as his connection to the Tuscan landscape. And good food always takes centre stage – whether it is at the River Café or in the generous environment of Rogers's home. But nothing has been as important in his life as his synergetic relationship with Ruthie, his wife and companion for more than 30 years. Together they have created a context of creativity, curiosity, community and warmth that transcends the power of his work and ideas.

It was Ruthie who asked me, along with other friends and family, to come up with one word to summarise my sense of Richard on the occasion of his seventieth birthday, a decade ago. I immediately returned to the noble Tuscan Oak – the *Quercus frainetto*. For me, Richard's physical presence, personality and demeanour mirror the groundedness, reliability and continuity of this enduring species, reflecting a sense of self-assuredness and optimism that is both infectious and comforting.

The Rogers family, portrait by Alain Aguano

Selected Bibliography

Bryan Appleyard, *Richard Rogers: A Biography*, London 1986

Kenneth Powell, *Richard Rogers*, Zurich and London, 1994

Kenneth Powell, *Richard Rogers: Complete Works*, London, three volumes, 1995–2001

Kenneth Powell, *Richard Rogers: Architecture of the Future*, Basel and Boston, 2005

Kester Rattenbury and Samantha Hardingham, *Richard Rogers: The Pompidou Centre*, Abingdon, 2011

Richard Rogers, *Architecture: A Modern View*, London, 1990

Richard Rogers, Richard Burdett and Peter Cook, *Richard Rogers Partnership: Works and Projects*, New York, 1996

Richard Rogers, *Cities for a Small Planet: Reith Lectures*, London, 1997

Richard Rogers and Mark Fisher, *A New London: Two Views*, Harmondsworth, 1992

Richard Rogers and Anne Power, *Cities for a Small Country*, London, 2000

Rogers Stirk Harbour + Partners, *Richard Rogers + Architects: From the House to the City*, London, 2010

Frank Russell (ed.), *Richard Rogers + Architects*, London and New York, 1985

Nathan Silver, *The Making of Beaubourg: A Building Biography of the Centre Pompidou*, Cambridge, Mass. and London, 1997

Deyan Sudjic, *New Architecture: Foster, Rogers, Stirling*, London, 1986

Deyan Sudjic, *The Architecture of Richard Rogers*, London 1995

Robert Torday, Richard Rogers Partnership and Ana Peco, *Richard Rogers*, Barcelona, 2006

Urban Task Force, *Towards an Urban Renaissance*, Abingdon, 1999

Urban Task Force, *Towards an Urban Renaissance: Executive Summary. The Report of the Urban Task Force*, Abingdon, 1999

Urban Task Force, *Towards a Strong Urban Renaissance*, Abingdon, 2005

Luis Vidal, *Richard Rogers*, Madrid, 2011

Photographic Acknowledgements

Index

This book is also published in a limited edition of 65 copies, each of which includes a print: *Zip-Up House*, 1968. Offset lithograph with hand colouring on 300 gsm Splendorgel paper, 16 x 22 cm, signed and numbered by Richard Rogers. Edition size: 50 plus 15 artist's proofs.